ARRIVAL AT ELSEWHERE

ARRIVAL AT ELSEWHERE

Curated by Carl Griffin

Published 2020 by Against the Grain Poetry Press
againstthegrainpoetrypress.wordpress.com

Cover images from OnlyGFX.com

ISBN 978-1-9163447-2-3

Printed by ImprintDigital.com

Contents

Introduction

Earlier this year, pictures emerged of a cruise ship quarantined after a passenger who had not long disembarked was tested positive for coronavirus. Passengers still on board were made to stay in their cabins, which led to the pictures: abandoned arcade rooms, an empty cinema, communal areas with no interaction. More than 3,000 people remained on the cruise ship, yet not one picture showed any sign of life.

As a poet, it is natural to explore the life around us, although not always natural to explore the obvious, immediate events. But from the moment these ghost ships could have become every day life, to the moment they did, I wanted to explore the change that was taking place.

In late March, I decided to reach out to other poets, suggesting a book-length poem I would compose from whatever fragments or poems they have written during the Covid-19 period. The scale of the impact of the coronavirus, and the fact that the book would raise money for charity, caused a positive reaction. Poets from the UK and USA, and a few other countries, sent me just under 400 pages worth of work.

My instinct was to make an account of the emotions generally brought about by the virus, rather than focusing too much on the physical changes, the social distancing, the rainbows in windows, the clapping for nurses. I preferred the poems/fragments which, on the face of it, seemed to be about something else, just as a person fully caught up in the lockdown period may have discovered things about their own individual life that they hadn't noticed before.

When I cut out the best fragments and began to spread them out on my dining table, the table quickly filled, and I still had loads of fragments to make room for. I held on to a piece of advice one of the contributing poets, John Sewell, had sent to me a few weeks before: "In my experience, what starts to look utterly impossible to pull together suddenly finds a way through which seems, in retrospect, inevitable." I repeated that mantra to myself, and read every fragment over and over, slotting them into this section, that section, until a few patterns emerged that I could use as my starting point. I can also confirm the last line of John Sewell's advice, which read: "That is such a beautiful moment".

The lines from this long poem are taken from, or inspired by, the poems or fragments sent by the poets. It was rare that I would use a whole poem, without mixing it up a bit, because I wanted each person's work, including my own, to go on a new journey. Some poets were not happy with this, and withdrew their work. As poetry is a very personal business, it can be unnerving when other poets re-stitch your words. But if I was to get a long poem, made from 97 poets, plus myself, and two extra editors, to read cohesively as possible, this had to be done. I chopped lines, or changed things around, while simultaneously attempting to retain as much as possible of the original character of each contribution. In some cases, I had to interpret or rewrite a poet's lines to fit the book, rather than use their words directly. These lines are still attributed to the relevant poet. If you like a certain section and wish to read the full poem those lines were taken from, all these poems will no doubt appear in the poets' future collections, and you can see which poet wrote what in the bios section. Lines attributed to myself are either taken from my own poems written during the pandemic, or are filler lines, connecting one fragment or section to the next.

This is an experimental, collaborative poem that was organized, written and edited in around six months and does not claim to be the voice of the pandemic. A poem which will raise a few pounds for NHS Charities Together, while giving future readers a little insight into the emotional obstacle that was Covid-19.

Carl Griffin

Publisher note

When the idea for this book was pitched to us it was still fairly early in the global Covid-19 pandemic. We were all still probably in a state of shock. All locked down, uncertain what was happening – we certainly felt we had landed in a new place. All three of us, like many poets, were unsure how to creatively assess this new situation. That's why we wanted to support this book. A collaboration of sorts, a creation of a road through all the work of poets who contributed to its making and a maker who has sensitively crafted this winding path of a poem from all our tongues. We are happy to support this work and its intention to support the NHS.

Abegail Morley, Karen Dennison and Jessica Mookherjee
Against the Grain Poetry Press

to everyone affected by the Covid-19 pandemic –

in aid of NHS Charities Together

Arrival at Elsewhere

The day is an occasion because
the diner at a roadside café table

reminds me of someone who is not
my dead mother nor my dead father.

The woman, in a skin-tight,
ankle-length dress, and high-heeled

silver sandals, who looks as if
she'll give birth any minute,

cradles a toddler in her arms,

resting him on the convenient
shelf of her jutting belly.

What cannot be taken away?
Putting down her homemade sandwich,

she shows me a picture she has just taken
of a lone deer wandering

across the carriageway.
Did he make it? I ask.

She nods to the empty road

but all I can see is a closed café
with a lady eating at its table.

What a letting go this Lent has been,
my appetite not deferred

but dead; my knife not sharpened
to a sheen but snapped instead.

The solution for this extended sabbath:
to screenshot the reticent wild

until our spare batteries go flat

or our phones are damaged
by the touch of too many fingers.

When this is all over
we'll go to where the windflowers

grow like fallen stars
along the river's edge, among

the mossy boulders, and see
how their night-eyes close.

She is not telling me, but her children.

Why have you never had children?
people often ask a childless woman,

as if one person's life does not carry
enough worth. A stone's throw from us

is a field with a dead well,
the shaft buried beneath long grass,

and in the corner is a frayed rope,
minus a swing, bound to a magnolia limb.

In this stillness, whose face

would ever be looking back?
A parent has branches

that make a canopy above your gaze.
Beside her, you will only see

the sky in glimpses.
Poking out of the hedgerow,

a sign says *Free Wheelbarrow*.
The wheelbarrow's gone.

I'll come back tomorrow for the seeds.

Today, I stopped to look at you,
beautiful world I cannot touch,

your paths cordoned off beyond this path,
and this field – the first grave

I have seen with a spruce
growing through it, the roots

inside the coffin, the death
of a human. Beautiful world,

I cannot touch you enough.

A word from a single
cotyledon in the cracked path:

you had no idea, it says,
how fast everything could change.

All of this is peaceful; anxious;
itchy on the surface of itself.

We long to scratch it, to enter
the valley where the deer assemble

to some beckoning forbidden to us.

Walking my regular walk along Birdcage
Lane, I am noticing the green leaves

of cherry, alder, lime and chestnut
unfolding with utmost precision,

ridged with ribbing and serrations,
the miraculous smallness of them.

Transform me, a homeless man
in The Gap once asked, his smile

incandescent as a late-century Christ,

*into a magnolia, blown
to pieces.* We realise,

now our eyes are open,
that things will never be

the same. A philosopher might say:
from one day to another, they never are,

and you never are. As if
in the pause of us, Spring is beginning.

As if it had been waiting for us

to be somewhere else…
Only, somewhere else, a place

called Elsewhere has turned up to stay:
here, estranged, or us estranged in it.

The homeless man who lives by the footbridge
seems to have abandoned his bender:

the shelter of groundsheets, space blankets,
frail metal armature, left to collapse in the rain.

Nascent pools, that make themselves

from floodwater off the ridge,
have taken his bed. The world planted

everything early. Now I watch
the mulch for movement, for augury

and largesse – cloak growth
with protective nets and fleece.

I'm less than eager at the prospect
of optimism's mid-morning burial.

You love death. You get the spade.

The universe is winding down –
the bleating human heart

sinking into the soil
and ticking quietly –

and might that not be
what we need? My shadow follows me,

reminding me always of two things –
my loneliness, and my loneliness.

I am carrying nothing. I am carrying myself.

*Wilderness in the soul can promise
assuagement*, said the painter,

and, on the map of her city,
darkness became light

and light became inhalation.
The opposite of faith is certainty.

Azaleas, bleeding hearts, tulips
turn the act of shaking

into a green animal.

I take a little path I have not tried before –
there are so many around here.

It goes down to a creek. On a leaf,
a dragonfly, a wing-equipped splinter

with jet-black military markings,
weighing nothing, is perched stock-still

in the centre of a silence
that feels as if it has just been

vacated by a deity.

If life is on hold, hold aging too.
Even the energetic youngsters,

having reached the peak,
are out of breath. They gasp,

looking around. I gasp that they made it.
The valleys are filled

with others making for the top,
and others like me gazing

blindly up at them.

Among toad-blistered leaves
of the foxglove, I watch her.

In pink slip and running shorts
she stands on the pinnacle

of Ragleth hill, arms raised,
a lightning rod

out above the valley.
Down here, beside me,

there's just a stump,

with no energy or direction,
without a scrap of green.

The stump hates natural light,
but in amongst its shock of twigs

is a pair of arms, rigid,
outstretched, aching to pull

me or whoever acknowledges it
into itself, its roots; a blistered runner

finding a second wind.

The faults are in my perception:
I see the area about me, wild garlic

and ground elder, the climbing roses,
limestone cliffs, but each part seems apart,

as if it is alone. I cannot agree
with how the consonants go with the vowels,

how plants may feel the pain
of outcrop, how the river's fullness

qualifies the trailing bough of ash,

how beech buds hold the pattern
of the water's shape.

I've seen you many times
but not like this.

The signal flickers, dwindles, dies.
Between us, distance grows like weed.

Shapes and shades and patterns
in the flowers you brought –

the varieties never reach an end.

This is what the wilderness is up to:
it rushes to its own destruction.

The waters run, eroding roots
and riverbanks, carving

the river's straightness into curves, forcing
the new meander. The cattle

move in concert with their pastures,
straining makeshift borders.

Still, I'm afraid –

afraid to think
there are no limits, or

we don't know what
to place a limit on.

How often have you dreaded
a butterfly effect, and swatted

the fluttering flight
away from the picnic?

And now a bat flies there.

Fine weather's a false positive.
We can see more clearly

through the atmosphere
but what we see is unreal.

Everything seems disjointed,
paths lead nowhere, large barns

block our passage. The cows and horses
may be real or decorations, put there

to distract. I've been looking

through a sweetshop window
at pink-blossom pear drops,

sugar mice, lemon-sherbet poppies.
The windowpane is misted.

Nose to the plate glass window
of a crisis, the thing,

if single thing it is,
too close and wide to see –

only to see through,

the way we see through glasses
with our face masks on – my breath

too hot, fogging the pane,
so we see little but the misting: our

own worry-sweat turning to chill
in every droplet. Finger-scribe

big blunt letters in the fog; write
S P R I N G. Watch a character

pucker at the edge and start to weep.

In the dark, interior rooms
of the body's hidden dimensions,

meetings are taking place:
not forbidden press conferences

or illegal holidays, but life and
death meetings where heart and mind

decide on the balance of powers,
the conscience together with impulses

hatching how hope might be maintained.

The darkness in the room crackles with static,
the greater mind in regular telecom

to maximise survival capabilities.
The muscles of the dank air flex

and the room's dimensions strain and shift.
I can hear it like the wind in the trees,

the susurrus filling the lungs
of birch and ash, thin and laboured

like an after gasp, the smoker's wheeze

that yet persists after thirteen years.
The introvert is so remote in the interior

there is a risk he will mislay himself
and never get his bearings back.

It is a day so still I hear, too, the creeping
of the moss. Beauty hurts, as much as pain:

both ride a long-drawn breath.
A child has carved a heart in a stone.

It sits at the roadside, tree-lit, not beating.

Some dreamscapes come to me:
the sea-less shore, its isolated figures

trailing robes across the sand,
the wind picking up and toying with

wool clots on barbed wire fencing
that separates the crofts.

The streets are abandoned. Trees
are breaking up the concrete

to push through empty pavements.
Someone is living in the ruined homestead

at the bottom of the garden.
Our new neighbours have not yet

announced themselves.
Why is the sea so far out?

I always used to see it here, a great
restlessness simmering beyond the sand.

On campus, even the hardest thing
is a sponge, glistening with world.

Concrete steps
of the white veranda in the sun,

scrolled ironwork
and glass roof. Clematis –

or some other creeper, not yet in leaf,
wrapped around the stanchions –

curls up towards the roof,

like a puzzle of wiring pulled out
from some machine and left unsolved.

Until denied, we do not know
our need, how we crave

touch, hands that reach out
to embrace, to make connection,

to have and to hold.
There's a rustle – a starling

waddles on the campus lawn,

slim, upright, glossy
black. As he turns, the light

catches, petrol-blue,
and you can just spot

his paler companion, keeping
to the rough edge of the grass,

and, further ahead, a wagtail,
pecking along then exploding

into flight, barely a yard

above the green, all at angles –
a tilt, yaw, tailspin,

a tiny fighter jet.
We are still out of touch.

They haven't seen the aliens land:
there will be science fiction,

new speeches, fresh conspiracies.
I'm reminded of *A Quiet Place*,

a movie, if life is not a movie,

about living silently as aliens swoop in
and kill at any tiny sound, and I realise

I'm not always putting my hearing aid in.
Through French windows

at the back of the veranda,
in the seminar room

beside grey plastic chairs
stacked upside-down on tables,

beneath the university slogan

bouncing around a blue screen,
I notice a forgotten whiteboard

and, on it, in neat blue marker:
Worry Stones, Support, Reasonable

Adjustments. The eaves
lend the lawn a long shadow,

a pause from elsewhere.
Up on the roof, around a little dome,

birds chatter like a Geiger counter.

Outside the National Gallery,
sixty lauded works of art begin

their journey to Tokyo's Western
Art exhibition. Through a split

in the tarpaulin, Van Gogh's
sunflowers stare at me,

as if this gallery is an extension
of their vase. They won't make it:

if everywhere was a place,

even that would close:
so too the campus, the art museum.

In galleries, at least, we recognise
that the objects are untouchable,

paintings, relics, reclining nudes,
the beauty, decadence. Golden leaf frames,

red braided rope; we gradually accept
even the trimmings are out of reach.

Now we know to keep our distance,

the trick is
not to lose touch.

Not that there's anything to touch,
just curious animals returning,

foxes in the square, stags in the metro,
peregrine falcons taking flight

from the tower of Riverside Church,
their cries crowding the altar.

On the chemist's roof, a carrion crow,

like a beaked plague-doctor,
is waiting for his work to start.

And when work starts,
it's as if an invisible snow

has fallen in the human quiet,
streets empty enough

that we can walk through
the middle of town

and step aside

when a car enters sight. Peacefulness
below the level we're accustomed to.

Three unempowered men –
no jobs, no homes –

sit outside Tom's Pizzeria,
closed now and up for sale.

How are you, man?
When this is over,

we're gonna go get a drink

at The Craftsman.
I'll buy the first round.

I was in the same pub
on the very last night.

There were people there I knew well
whom I might not see again.

I'm so tired of hearing
about your anxieties,

about anxiety.

In geography class, I began to travel,
across the schoolroom map,

through pages of the atlas.
The world became a treasure

house of cities, languages, landscapes.
I could imagine a stroll

by the rivers of Germany,
between trees in the Black Forest,

tossing snowballs in the Alps.

Now, there's no one at the Champs-Élysées,
the piazza of San Marco,

the spice market of Istanbul,
the greasy spoon of High Street.

But there is someone here,
at least, ourselves,

at another magnolia, counting
a thousand petals, fallen

from the introverted chandelier.

Clacking canes against cobbled
walkways, the elderly look

through acrylic face masks.
They are not in galactic space,

not in a laboratory,
piecing together elements of a cure,

but beneath a row of red maples
while a refrigerator truck parks,

humming the dead's silence.

At the cricket club,
the old matchboard reads

"VS". between two blanks.
What are we up against?

Things don't know the names
we give to them. A coot

is not aware that it's a coot.
And pain doesn't know

it is hurting us.

Paddling in the shallow water
by the shore, I watch an elderly woman

shuffle along the beach, her bare feet
pitching into the sand, forcing her to right herself

with every step. She wears black gloves,
a purple linen dress, a pointed wicker hat.

She's a working woman. I know this,
as does everyone else, from the bamboo

balancing on her shoulder.

At one end of the wood hangs
a metallic bowl, a portable barbeque

barely lit; at the other, swings a bag
of uncooked corncobs.

Someone gestures and she drops
to her knees, retrieves a box of matches

from her pocket. The barbeque lit,
she undresses a fresh cob then places it

on the grill, above red-black coals.

I dunk my head under the cold waves
and swim away from the sun-loungers,

the slipped towels and sun-burnt bodies,
from the bare-foot grey-haired woman

painting the corn with honey-herb sauce
I think I smell while immersed underwater.

When I surface, the current
has pulled me a short distance

from where I started.

A construction site is in full swing
on this patch of shore; a new hotel,

no doubt. A sweating foreman, in trousers
and shirtsleeves, points his clipboard

for the attention of the shirtless
construction worker beside him,

not at steel girders protruding
out of the ground, but at two mongrels

mating on the sand.

Somewhere, a cruiser
is patrolling the North Sea.

You imagine it
passing the headland,

like your own dream of waking,
just turning over, not quite conscious,

flattening tempestuous waves
in the darkness, there,

beyond the shore lights.

We are waiting for the liner
to dock. A crowd has gathered,

wondering what it might bring.
This experiment mining to find

all that is broken is breaking us.
In the sea where white boats bob,

inner tubes sink and no one is rescued.
Like the pair of ducks mirrored

in the lake, we drink ourselves.

Half-way across the River Styx,
Charon asks for twenty bucks.

But I left my money on the bank
of the river, and I want another chance

to wander into the caves
furthest from surfers and gulls,

furthest from sailors cut adrift.
Charon keeps rowing, you can hear the oars.

This isn't the moment to dither.

A pink moon, she says,
as she watches through clouds moving together.

A spectacle in the trees, a lucent brilliance
like hanging silk

or a wine glass filled with chardonnay.
A pink moon drawing close,

as if it knows that Earth now needs a mother
like the mother who comes to the child

who wakes up frantic.

The Eiffel Tower balances on Montparnasse rooftops
from the west windows so you keep them unshuttered

though every night is moonless either way,
and wide roads are so emptied of traffic by its mass

that when rushing from Javel to make the morning train
its glare can burn as if you've stared at the sun,

and it is sextant and Polaris both in how it points
every path to itself: the spire, the vaulted space beneath,

the peddler priests and their plastic reliquary.
Suddenly, when I can't see it, it's not because I'm at

the prism base gazing up through geometric layers,
sky upon iron upon sky upon iron upon sky,

it's because it's gone – the iron shaping the sky, the light,
the spell – all gone. And, in days, hours even, the city

will begin the tiny acts of erasure all grievers do:
understanding the dark; taking detours; forgetting.

I cry over the spatchcocked body,
the delicate speckling

on its upturned belly, the translucent
green of the rest of it,

and then my eye travels to the hole
in its head, a young frog,

and I wonder if I have lived too long
with an entrapment of feelings

which allowed the garden's growth

of an illusion of safety
conveyed by the absence of people.

I used to fear the dark as palpable,
not luminous at its interior,

but learnt to know its inner dialect,
like just today these shocking pink anemones

are joined by frilly indigo and red
I'd forgotten all winter underground.

Their extravagant colour swatch of silks

are like the patterns thrown
across the comfy kimono

we confuse for the wearer's skin.
All night I'd listened

to a low drone of planes
as muffled sky traffic, and familiarised

myself with plans conceived for the next day
as though already done, and learnt in this

the art of being ahead and not behind,

rotation into day, and knew in time
sleep would return, but be different

for knowledge gained of its alternative,
the comfort of communion with the self,

and went outside at 6a.m., the sky
orange, turquoise and black, and they were there,

anemones, a solo purple one
new to the rest, affirming its passage

out of the dark into rewarding light.

Violets speckle a small patch
of grass, a purple rash

spreading slower
than the eczema scabs on my hand.

Before the move, I never
had a garden for life

to thrive in, with branches
to fall from.

In my last house, primroses

were everywhere; they'd spread
onto the lawn, and my first cut

of the grass would wait
until they'd finished flowering.

Here, they're clustered
under an apple tree.

It's Spring, even if
the tree is slow into leaf. I can still see,

between its branches, the usual

view of the hills. Sprouting,
burgeoning, mating; the fertile time.

Tulips are out. These are spectacular:
petals red opening to gold

take me back to old Amsterdam,
to the seventeenth century,

where these would be worth a fortune –
the gold streaks caused by a virus.

Clipping the hedge while people disappear

seems a trite action.
But, although travellers drop

at every port of call,
planting seed wherever the jet lands,

we spend so many hours in the garden
that any tangle is our own.

A garden that has stopped
hammering us with what we know,

and surprised us.

A sparrowhawk is circling,
listening for fledglings, or a sound

like the sound I have made
as I've listened to the dawn

chorus, every morning,
for the first time in my life.

I've heard that people can die
just because they've run out

of other things to do.

There are Japanese gardens
which model in miniature the stages

of pilgrimages, for those
unable to take them on.

Here, in my garden,
is an image of Scotland –

a birch, heather, a rock
and miniature conifer.

Walking round this and other epitomes,

I'm looking for my life,
which might be a pilgrimage.

My life is looking for me.
I'm noticing the crows

on the roof these days,
which focuses me on planting

to discourage them
from pecking out my eyes.

How like generals or dignitaries

they are, engaged
in their great office.

This, they declare, above small
suburban gardens, is their day

in the sun. If I could match that,
or another deftness – the way

the play-chase-and-squabble
of adolescent rats on the patio

twines with their twitch-perfect

nose for a new chance, and the Spring-
loaded life force that catapults them

into cover, their whisker-fine grip
on the balance of containment

and quest – I would be another species,
better suited for this harshness.

My daughter made a bouquet of gorse.
Harsh! I recoiled.

Yes and *not yes.*

It's true, gorse is a glove
of blood for any hand,

a paradigm of touch-me-not,
a keep-your-distance hedge,

but gorse endures, defends, fends off
the slightest touch.

A little bird lays splayed
beneath our hacked hedge:

an open-mouthed

strip of flesh and down,
gaping silently;

barely formed wings
outlined in veins and sinews.

I check that this is not
a coincidental arrangement of sticks

and garden centre grit.
I hadn't known there was a nest

until I chopped through it.

My mother talks to me
from her own garden,

her hands full of biscuits for the dog,
nuts for the bird box,

as well as the phone. *There's a robin
which comes into the kitchen,*

she says. *It flies through the house,
around the kitchen and out the front door.*

Do you think it's always the same robin?

There are quite a lot of robins.
Her garden is full of birds and dogs

buried under the ash tree.
And there are ashes under the ash tree.

Yesterday, she says, *the robin didn't come.*
It was fine, all the doors and windows open.

There was a robin at the bird box
but I don't think it was my robin.

Perhaps it will come tomorrow.

My own small joy
crept up

after the morning of immediate tears,
the crying into the soup.

It was something I wasn't sure
I could allow in,

my friend's boy skateboarding
the middle of our street,

how he turned

his white helmeted head
and waved.

Something about clouds
is troubling you today.

It is to do with how much
of your thinking

they used to take up. No more.
Away they fly,

bright rags, then grey sheep,

then the cloud is just a kite
wheeling over Weston Lane,

the poor side of town.
Not being governed.

I roam to the decking, above the bowl
of garden. A place for contemplation.

Carrion, always on the look-out
for carrion, a cook's offal

or the bones of a pet.

It has become all right for me to tell
everything about me:

it's as if there are two of me,
the broken

nocturnal endangered species
caught in bulb light weeping

and this other, newer animal.
Just as rare, but this one will hold

your gaze, has learnt to enjoy pain

as microbes do, thriving iridescently
under poisoned outflows.

This new animal daily surprises itself,
mimicking the sound of humans,

has a new way of walking –
the art of avoidance

is in the grace of the swerve
to the left or the right,

that speaks of the need for space.

In my Dürer dreams, the sea fell
from the sky. It once held stars

above the mountains. Its shoal
was obverse and mirror-wise creatures

who worshipped a darker moon,
and dreamt of waking as the people

who dreamt them up. Sensing new darkness
emerge below itself, the sea buckled,

gushed a waterfall a thousand miles wide.
Is the sea's light ample for all shores?

I don't know if I can hold the slickness
of its fish, but light hits me still

and sinks. Doves, no longer the flood's
plucked apples, drown. In mid-air.

How can this sea make me a stone
yet be so hard itself? Am I a new gull?

Someone is always boiling
a kettle, an elaborate

torture of temporal
continuity, a signal device.

The house feels fresh,
with more space to walk,

with a scent I can trust.
The dog barks at the door.

She hasn't been out yet.

It's always been a dog's life,
and if a deity ever entered

my shaggy existence
it was only the unlettered moon

to whom I howled all those nights.
What does faith boil down to

but a bowl on the tiled floor
we only remember when there's nothing

closer to feed us.

They've logged the hillside of conifers.
Only the scent is left standing,

this uphill path so different now,
and so much at a loss.

There's no one here but us
to see the chanterelles

which have sprung up on the trail.
Even in the village, walking the dog,

you become conscious of how different

the weather is now. You raise
your voice an octave to say

nice day to strangers swerving off
the path to pass obligatory.

To say *nice day* is to beg
them to ignore the black, shaggy cloud

embodied in that new breed
of language that trails,

tangles and trips everyone's feet

despite – or because of – its lack
of any muzzle or lead.

I remember the wooden cross
in the church grounds with a crown

of barbed wire. We approach it
across wet grass – the shape is atavistic,

four points like a body,
the raised head and quiet legs, still.

It's a long, slow wrinkling we walk on.

I think my son cannot tell between
real cross and apocryphal –

I still enter these uncertainties.
The longer the trail behind,

the less it stays behind. It curves –
not social distancing, not that

awkward choreography of swerve,
no, but as if a tuck is taken in fabric,

a sudden loop, a little lateral leap.

Inside the church, mass is cancelled,
one contagion yielding to another.

Recent looks far away
and long ago. Far away turns

into here, now, so you leap back.
Distant conversations surface.

If memories can live in an element
that lets them dive and sink,

these rise like swimmers.

Under the cross are dog violets
in various stages of growth.

I once took three to study
at home. Indoors, with my glasses on,

I noted the pale opening
in the middle lower petal, the stripes

like retinal veins. An organ
sits idle in its moorings,

its music dormant in the pipes.

The church walls have niches,
left from the medieval cells

where anchorites lived. Hermits,
who climbed into living tombs.

Anachoresis: a medical word meaning
the transportation of foreign bodies

via blood. A Greek word, meaning living
away from others, self-sequestering,

embracing the solitary place.

I pick two daisies, three heads
of lesser celandine, a sprig of forget-

me-not. The bluebells have the strongest scent,
sure of its tone, a narrow band

of sweet exchange
with the brain receptors.

Is this what insects fall for?
Or is it the shape, six petals

curling upwards like an inaccurate octopus.

We get to the flats, a liver-shaped plain
of gorse thickets, groundwater ponds,

sloped football pitches.
We've walked it for years

but were always walking through it,
on the way to somewhere.

Now we dwell amongst its trees,
hear a song like a winnowing hinge

and follow it quietly through the gorse,

finding a greenfinch calling from a bramble.
And in-between the tumble and snaggle

of gorse bushes, butterflies, everywhere we turn:
speckled wood, brimstone, painted lady.

We come to an oak that sits alone
in the centre of a glade

where three paths meet, its branches
low and long and scoring

the air like lightning bolts.

Heading home, our son and daughter
notice a change in the lane.

It is quiet again. Only a breeze
and the aroma of sheep faeces

and something even the dog
doesn't want to sniff out,

the dirt track mobile, unquiet
in the declining light.

No one stops to look back.

This is now how days wring
their hands on the slopes above us,

a slow dressing into woodland greens,
an anxious spreading of boughs,

a concentrated building of nook
and niche, a re-peopling of habitats.

Or this is how we imagine things
unfolding in the halted evolution,

while we are locked in our homes.

In the evenings, a kind of dread set in.
Was it possible that the paradigm

for their entire life together would change,
the gyroscope drop to a stop

on the green felt table
that had been the centre of their lives,

cigar smoke rising above his white collar?
That was a thing he could now contemplate,

as the brandy thickened in his forehead,
a thought he could only entertain

when the fate of the human race was at stake,
and his little life wasn't all there was

to be lost. She had started to sicken,
the ivory slope of her nose reddened

at the sides. The boy too, had a leaden cough.
Was this their great displacement?

Deathwatch beetles,
such a distinctive tick

to their borings. Their collective,
tiny strengths causing us

to poke at what's exposed,
begin a fall of timber crumbs.

We hear these omens clearly now,
with the cars gone, traffic lulled,

and wake to find them

speckled upon carpet
and our books. Our child

collects curled husks, prehistoric
in the pink of her palm.

We kneel before her fingers,
thankful she was dreaming

when they came down
from the beams.

Let us thrive beneath this truss.

Anxiety. Technicalities
of midmorning. The small talk

of dreams and waking.
Long conversations

between flesh and aching light.
The fierce birds of day.

Someone is awake
in the new house. Someone stands.

Someone sings aloud.

We all learn how to make things so clean
they can never be dirty again.

How did we manage before?
Dirt now cannot affix to surfaces

or coagulate in divots.
Even the air gleams.

Anything with a mass is cleaned
at a sub-atomic level. The dirty

is transported to industrial estates.

I want to be first discoverer
of that village in the shadow

of a mountain where not everything glistens,
where bedsheets are seamy

and books smell of gum agar,
where a stranger, with crescents of dirt

under her nails and jam-dangled knots
in her hair, smiles at me,

and does not edge back.

I hoover the dust
off the 4kg dumbbells

that have languished under the desk
for years, attempt goblet squats

and cross-body hammer curls
by the large lounge window, looking out

across long back gardens that stretch
into sunlight. The snake sloughing off

another skin gets to begin again.

I miss the pool, exercise
without feeling you're exercising,

the shock of submersion,
the counting of the lengths,

even leisure centre tiles, chlorine,
finding a vacant locker

under fluorescent lights.
Before we return to the brink,

the crack between us will widen.

Life has turned itself upside down,
like a snow globe, ephemerally

wobbling on the uneven side,
the transparent side, its vignette

simply a man in a house
in a blizzard of blossom.

From cellar steps or kitchen stool,
from the garage of missing tools,

I've made this blossom my hibernaculum.

The sun blurs to a cold wind
that blows horse chestnut flowers

in through the window.
They land at my feet as I lift

the weights, releasing a pollen scent
from white petals with pink swirls

like raspberry-ripple ice cream.
A magpie arrives in my long garden,

lands in the tree with a crash.

Today will be a sweet pollen,
not the foul-smelling kind.

Awake to thought –
I'm not the problem, it's the lens;

I'm sure I'll die surprised by light.
I know there is no future here

but I do exist.
I understood life

to be performing.

Tautologically my point-
lessness is centred

on the mind receiving
its own flat lidless stare.

Supposing you brought the light
inside the body. Supposing you drank

the good disinfectant. Supposing life
were living, literal, or there.

I can see I do not know.

While we are away,
the trees agree

to bloom unruly
ribbons in their rows.

This light will bear repeating.
When I sleep, it doesn't work.

In this stillness, the body
is taking place. I have felt

a hand in the small of my back.

Sometimes I pace the floor,
and my roaring startles the crows

on everyone's roof. My partner
would let me out, but is afraid

of what I'd do with the sudden freedom.
Then sometimes, this is a gift.

I remember Grandma Wanda, who feared
the exam she was to retake

in 1939. There was no exam.

In thirty years, when I sit by the fire
and my grandchild asks what I did

during the crisis, I would like to say
the silence was so magnificent

I sprang into it, I pulled myself
by my own ears into its blessing,

my only fear not spending each
gifted hour wisely in case

you would come, just as you have.

In this change, in this room,
I am free to feel what I feel.

I only grieve for how isolated
we already were.

How many of us have always
had our doors or windows shut,

locked in the house
of our body?

Existence is lock-down.

Do we spend our lives
how we spend our hours?

Mortality cannot be glimpsed
between walls as solid as these.

We climb the stairs, and at the top
floor window we look back

over the rough track
and between the sweep of greens and browns

can almost see our own footsteps,

and at the window of the house
across the way, another face.

It is not possible to waste time
though it, in time, wastes us.

An empty day is still complete,
its glass brim full –

let it touch our lips.
All that amounts to a lot

is a loch stumbled on in Wester Ross.

There is another world out there,
with a real sun

that warms my shirt,
new leaves and yellow flowers.

A chaffinch hops branches
as he sings our exhumation.

Will every meal now be delivered,
foraged in forgotten acres

and prepared with someone else's sunburn?

Today's menu has gone up
in the smoke of ground cinnamon,

at the click of the last jar's cap.
Start with herbs. Betony,

fresh from the garden,
lovage and hyssop, a touch

of lemon balm. Tonight,
woodcock poached in milk,

cooked bone marrow,

hare cured in brine.
A partridge rubbed with tansy,

a hedgehog on the fire.
There are ways to be buried

without the ground seizing
what is its own. The heart

pleads with you to let it out,
promises to stay apart from all

the other hearts.

In my Dürer dreams, a crab
hoists its eyes and skitters down

a flooded rabbit-hole. Roofs unslab.
Fanning a nauseating stench, we are found

trapped on doorsteps, posed and bound,
like supplicants to some very minor god

tasting for salt in rain, all sea and Cape Cod.
In every droplet are the lights of a metropolis.

You walk through the fine mesh of sleep,
part dreaming, part drifting, part drowned.

While seeing what was always there
but had passed unobserved,

sleep sweetly, sleep deeply, sleep sound.
In dreams, the storm is always shifting

until despair, so life-like, lifts.
Sleep until light comes around.

I see all the world from my window:
three red brick buildings

spelling out the shape of a waiting adder.
Distant farmland is trimmed by a chimney.

Sunbathing, a bald man's skin
merges with the walls.

If I were to jump, I'll fall
into the arms of nothing,

better known as everything.

My niece is surviving
by pretending it's always her birthday.

Here comes a photo to my mobile
of today's outfit.

What I wouldn't give
to be wearing my party best,

clutching a sparkling glass
and talking to someone

about the gloriously mundane.

I long for the artificial willow
in my office.

I long for my office.
I ride about on any idea

that could be regarded as having a saddle
and all of every day

(this is what it boils down to)
I must be myself.

Isolation's trying to mould me.

I think my body onto fresh moors,
the distraction of air, damp

ground spoiling my shoes,
anything to tip me

back into the world as it used to be,
anything to shake me

from the person I'm becoming.
My floor becomes wilder

by the day.

I visit art galleries inside my television
where the bored artist razes

his own house down. Bust doors,
smashed windows. Like a barn.

Twitter people are adding up
the number of days

since someone last touched them.
Thousands of years

vibrate in my palm.

For the tenth time today,
my partner's opening two notes

of Gershwin's Rhapsody in Blue
are followed by a crashing, wistful descent

into the resolve.
Then the whole show kicks in.

This month, I have heard it
a hundred times. I'm going

to keep listening. I'm going Gershwin.

Somewhere in our library
may be a sentence

that makes sense of it all
but every page is blurry.

An ex-girlfriend has sent a message
to remind me of the paperback

she gave me, that tells it all,
about her, about then:

about now,

and that's the reason
she needs it back.

I take down a slew of books
I haven't read from the shelves.

I use cancelled tickets
to cultural events

as bookmarks. Everything
I have read, and written

has been irrelevant.

Outside this life, you're playing hide-
and-seek with me, peeling the backbone

of shadows from their stretch.
You speak of my strings,

hinges, unbraided hair; tiny drill holes
through fingers and wrists ache

in the cold, and my voice,
rising from the slim cord of spine,

pools in the air like a bruise.

The play is unscripted –
I don't know where it ends

or begins. I have lost
the shape of my days,

of my clothes, of all
that is holding me up.

I don't know if this is wrong.
I only know it's true.

I don't miss you.

In this doll's house –
its wallpaper and tiny carved beds –

I slam the timber door,
and it loosens from its hinges.

In Act II, I raise my arms,
move across this vacant stage

in my Spring outfit, poke the front row
with a stick. I've lost my audience,

but at the back, in light

you're shuffling, you're watching,
and, thirty seconds from now,

my dance will reach the end
of its dark alley and fade

with the stage lights. You'll stay
in your seat long after my curtain call

just to touch the horror of me
as I exit, strings tangling.

I don't miss people.

I haven't felt the days drag their anchors,
nor pass in full sail with a fair wind,

but I've watched swifts switch the evening
between slow motion and fast forward

on the merest whim of wing.
Nor have I honed patchwork or priesthood

with the weeks yawning wide and warm
beneath me, but I've learned this language

of whisper, watering my house plants.

I haven't sought out miracle cures
but have taken pills of each colour,

swallowed every small defeat whole,
and scrubbed my hands of every touch.

I've walked out in the wolf hour
to wash myself in showers of song,

buried my grief in the sky again.
I have drunk deep of the brightest star,

and will be bleeding light for years.

I'm looking at things much
as I've always looked at them –

on screens, pages,
but through a different frame.

As a new, peripheral choreography
cuts through casual encounters,

the eye is more attuned
to encroachment, edges, metaphor.

We are sick of metaphors.

When the big ideas flew in
we made room for them

and fed them on dew.
Where is the dew now?

This standstill in the essence of our lives,
we drop through it into unfamiliarity.

As our worries whelm and mass
beyond what we can see, we brace

for whatever kind of resumption

may be possible, in continuity.
We've given up on edges

but our imprint is there
in the molecules of air

in homeopathic quantities.
We all have our demons.

Mine have surfaced after many years.
Just as metaphor underlies

all thought, our demons

underlie each action we take, every day
they live through our routines,

invisible but exercising control.
The main fear I have

is that I will always feel afraid.
Demons were once nocturnal,

breathing in darkness like fish
breathe in water. But nights now

are days that have no light.

Pharaoh's magicians kept an ace
up their sash, turning the River Nile

to blood, or wooden staffs to snakes,
bestowing life to a wax crocodile.

Heka masters, sorcerers, lector priests,
shaking temples with their secret arts,

could they have conjured this up,
the spike on the viral capsid,

this micrograph reminiscent of a halo?

Could they cast out its power
with their apotropaic forefingers?

The old ways are always the best,
and maybe that is how

we will remember this:
in the old way, yet

never as *the past*.
A wind runs down the stream

of the future. Here.

The hall is dark now,
a strip of light by the door.

Here's the mise-en-scène
for a film we might devise,

waiting for something
to happen, for hours

to unfold
like a lotus, soft

as these evenings.

There will be time,
all the time in the world,

to visit again the old books,
those lives you left,

vowing you would return,
time to meet again those friends

you loved, and missed
the moment their story closed.

So many years you want to live again.

On National Park crushed stone,
a brown bear is swiping at an abandoned

traffic cone whose reflective striping
and fluorescence has been abraded

by the dust. The bear knocks the cone
to the stone and moves on.

The jeeps haven't been seen
for days. Or heard. Or retreated from.

Another bear comes,
ambling on all fours.

With its teeth, it grips
the base of the dull cone

and, like a ranger, claws
the rangers' cone from underneath,

and, as if making good on the carelessness
of his neighbour, leaves it upright.

All I hear now is a wife
ransacking chest drawers

to dig-up unopened anniversary
floral paper boxes

of bars of neatly-packed soap:
a Pioppino mushroom

that adds moisture to the skin,
poppy seeds and sea salt

to exfoliate her flaking fingers.

How last-minute she once deemed
these gifts. Redundant novelties.

She unpacks them like aid kits,
and the open, angled bureau top

is fragranced with oil clouds
of cypress, coconut, ylang-ylang.

With a hand lathered with the minerals
and nutrients of a rainforest,

she switches off the bedroom light.

The neighbours on my street
are home tonight and every night.

All I see of them is the glow
of binged Netflix.

Their doorbells are navels
of galaxies in Hubble space.

I could shout. No one would hear
my voice but the Gordon Setter

beside me in the dark.

The night is a malady
disguised as patience.

I drop my dog's lead
and she scampers around a house

where skunks wait for other skunks
to love, and they love her not.

She has found her nose in the shadows.
Everything is the shade of shadows now,

and she's as transparent as the sound of her name.

The hand mirror I bought
six months ago is so cheap,

so poorly made, it no longer
reflects who I am.

I've forgotten how to clean
my teeth, or change into

my night shirt. The convolvulus
moon hangs in the sky

but I am facing the wrong way

and have forgotten how
to turn around.

For you, as for me,
the empire of silence advances,

the earth itself stays back:
I offer you a held breath,

stalled step, your milky body
lashed to distance like a star.

All mirrors are faulty.

And in all mirrors, reflections,
you notice another face

shadowing your own.
Where in the world… you ask it,

though it is the world.
Entirely other,

the world turns this way and that
and doesn't know you.

Sit down, it says. *Stay.*

Each time I get up it is still dark,
with that pallid glow.

We are hours from dawn. My lover
is asleep and no one knows I am awake.

The insomniacs are cursing
from their many rooms,

turning in sodden beds
or running a hand through tangly hair.

I take a paracetamol.

My Uncle Zoltán
had an eye for disasters.

He'd watch them passing
like a smear of crows

cursing at the failing light.
His gothic nature,

drunk on the melodrama,
sympathized with them.

He was facetious. Sometimes he was right.

First, we heard the back-door rattle,
then the catch on the downstairs

cloakroom window started to jiggle.
There was a banging on the wall,

and the dog whining in the scullery
when she heard the splintering of wood.

We tried to remember the Lord's Prayer.
The radio said to lie on the floor

and, if we could, limit our breathing.

"I was passed the plague by Graf Archibald
of Gröningen", wrote Uncle Zoltán.

"He sent it to me in a letter
and left me to pay the postage.

I hate second-hand plagues.
I bought my last from a highly

reputable antique dealer.
It had no practical use

but looked handsome on the mantelpiece.

I suffered terribly
with the Black Death. My hair

turned grey first, then white.
It was like old television,

no colour at all.
I was told they had a plaque

in the next village.
Who could resist that?

You may imagine my disappointment."

"I have lived in solitary quarantine",
wrote Uncle Zoltán. "A room

full of myself was deafening,
it was difficult to get a word in.

I have a three-piece plague suit
I have worn since 1351.

In those days, I had a servant
bring the plague in on a tray.

There has been a servant problem ever since.

I remember when doctors
wore bird masks to visit.

We put out seed for them.
How beautifully they sang.

And think of the eggs!
All my diseases have been fatal

but death has improved me at every turn.
I pop in and out of time

like a cuckoo from its clock."

On a night of a full moon, dream animals
return to feed us as best they can.

Eat the animals' gifts, or imagine them,
because imagination, too, is edible.

A tiger enters the house. I have no meat
for it except my flesh. Its mascara blends

with blood monochrome hues meshed in the sleet –
I borrow sexual contact from the clouds.

Margot decided to go to a restaurant
where she can order a dish she likes.

Margot can do this in a dream
where the restaurants are open.

Carlos dances in a fountain with a dama
who sings to the milonga on vinyl.

Carlos doesn't have to hold the shoulders,
in the dream, of a costume from his closet.

And already, legends ago,
old growth has been lumbered

and carted off
wherever Southern Pacific runs,

wavy marsh grasses
ripped out,

leaving a shadow
of yellow fever and tuberculosis

in rich, black giving topsoil.

Already a Mardi Gras flotilla
floats in early morning sunshine

as if to undo the day before,
paint and glitter in an uproar –

before or now – bacchanalia hanging
from eaves in the French Quarter,

but then plummets a novel virus
through our old racial memory

rolling back to the grey mounds

of smallpox blankets torched
by soldiers, ancestral loneliness

working its way down
through victims who were born

talking rumours of war, always
with arms around the shoulders

of the youngest,
crossing memory's land bridge

to another isolated side,

and already the old
wounds of desire return

as heart trouble, sugar, obesity,
blues, partying as anarchy,

and wet, wormy earth awakens
before a woeful all-seeing eye…

The presence of the plague
affects how I experience

being in my body.

Even the subtlest shift
in the weather, a sneeze or cough,

brings an internal inquisition:
am I really ill, how ill is this,

is death a missed pill away,
a walk round the block away?

I have overdosed my body
with Vitamin C.

And now the tree-pollen has arrived.

Are the insects done battering
at the glass? I have swept

and shaken their darkness away
but I crumbled, a trellis

falling from the wall.
How welcome the rain was

on the window this morning,
almost a month since it last fell,

now ubiquitous, surviving

its journey across the Pennines
to put out candles the neighbours

left burning on the outside sills.
Outside, a buffet of sicknesses

secrete in firm and airy pastry.
We can't leave the pastry alone.

Difference. We even had to put
the lights on. The cool grey.

Droplets static on the window

were nudged from their fastenings
by the newly fallen. They slip

like tadpoles down the pane, chicane
through bubbles of their sister-spawn.

Roof tiles gleam like brown leather,
now the world is more silent than ever

in its cocoon of cloud and water.
Even the birds

draw a relieved breath.

Oxygen is rationed.
A ceanothus tree blooms

outside the doctor's surgery.
My cyanosed fingers click

to a close-up clustered
with blue flowers –

closer, they are bronchioles,
branching to alveoli

inhale, exhale, inhale

I don't want the world to think
there's no one here at all.

Three times Odysseus tried to grasp
and hug his incorporeal mother.

Three times Aeneas tried to reach
and hug his father, who – also dead,

incorporeal – resisted touch.
We need the company of strangers

to make our own strangeness less.

I am full of others. Most
I have never known, though some

have familiar names and faces.
They appear on the half-landing,

in the half-light when wakefulness
begins eventually to slip its moorings,

when the bed, the darkness, the walls
are gone, replaced by something

fluid, unplanned.

Then the day's long hawsers
go slack. They drop

from the capstans,
are cast-off, and I am adrift

and the current is towards
the deep. I am immersed

in the crowd of the living
and the dead. They are all here.

I know their faces.

This could be a game.
One person hides,

the others seek.
The smaller the alcove,

the better. If others find
they too must join in. Soon,

everyone is hidden
cheek by jowl (or fin by gill),

packed, waiting for the ring to be pulled.

There's a cough in the wardrobe,
a dry cough, a cough with legs,

a kennel cough, a Romanoff cough,
a bring-out-your-dead cough.

The wardrobe feels hot.
It's wheezing, as if a fist

were beating on its door.
I hunt for a thermometer

although I know I haven't got one.

We have seen only each other
for eleven days. Our fevers

are low-grade and only one of us
coughs through the night.

The doctor upstairs
cannot calm her children.

When they trample the floors,
it sounds as if they're hammering

the lid onto a coffin.

My father still doesn't believe
anyone's in danger, while two

cancers grow inside him.
Surgery has been suspended

while they ready the wards
for patients beyond breath.

Like a spell, I list everyone
I want to save – repeat their names

while you sleep beside me.

I am noticed. I am overseen.
Down the surgery phone,

my doctor recommends B12 pills,
despite having told me

I am unable to absorb them.
The practice is shut.

Sometimes I sit in a chair
and shake with contagion,

then shake to the recovery position.

Steps to recovery:
first, there needs to be pain,

something to recover from.
For this person, it's a thumbtack-

type stab. *Right flank*,
they hear the doctor say,

while looking at an image of their insides,
not knowing why it hurts.

Second, wake to the less pleasant world,

one where this person must breathe
on their own, a rasping,

emotive catheter
that stays in the throat.

Right flank now pulse-pounds,
skin stretched over this hollow space.

Sewn from the inside,
these stitches will break down

like bodies in the ground.

If only illness sat on a wooden bench
beneath a golden acacia,

where a breeze has shaken the leaves
and misery has gone.

It could follow an amber flow.
In threads of honey tone,

photosynthesis could purify it
with water, light and nutrition.

Like the acacia, it could be healed by the sun.

At home, there is an extra stage,
a period when I can use propitiatory magic

pretending I am in control
of virus-particles, that I can shield myself,

telekinetically flick them to ash.
My hands crack from washing.

My skin seems to have aged – bruised
and scaled like dragon-skin.

These improvised palaces,

bolted together with fabrications
and the screws of home comforts,

have turned loose and tangled
like the disused wilderness.

Every night we can hear a dog
barking several streets away.

It is our dog. Next to us.
We lie in the endless dark

and do not fall asleep.

The disenchantment comes
to commandeer the night.

At dawn, we remember
the sea is out there somewhere,

then forget again. As for day,
what need of it without the night? And now

since there is no time like the present
we are waiting. It has always been this way.

How dependent we were on the light.
Now, whatever we touch is unremarkable

to the eye, peeling back until
there is nothing left to reveal.

Scraped and pocked, the solid surface we stand on
is also a series of tiny eruptions,

and every surface will burst its banks
where some of us are sleeping.

Biographies

Indran Amirthanayagam writes in English, Spanish, French, Portuguese and Haitian Creole. He has published nineteen poetry collections, including *The Migrant States* (www.hangingloosepress.com), *Sur l'île nostalgique (L'Harmattan, 2020)* and *Lírica a tiempo (Mesa Redonda, Lima, 2020)*. www.indranmx.com

Indran's lines appear on page 32, lines 11-13, lines 16-18.

Valerie Bence's latest collection, *Falling in Love with a Dead Man*, was published in 2019 by Cinnamon Press.

Valerie's lines appear on page 17, line 17, and page 18, lines 1-3.

Kathryn Bevis is Hampshire Poet 2020 and founder of The Writing School. In 2019 she won the Poets and Players competition, the Against the Grain competition, and was shortlisted for the Nine Arches Primers scheme. She is working towards her first collection.

Kathryn's lines appear on page 14, lines 14-16.

Stephen Bone's first collection, *In The Cinema,* appeared in 2014, followed by a pamphlet, *Plainsong* (Indigo Dreams) in 2018. A Hedgehog Press micro-pamphlet is due in 2020.

Stephen's lines appear on page 20, lines 9-11.

Jemma Borg's first collection, *The illuminated world* (Eyewear, 2014), won the inaugural Fledgling Award. She won the Ginkgo Ecopoetry Prize in 2018 and the RSPB/Rialto Nature and Place Competition in 2017, and recent publications include *The Poetry Review, Oxford Poetry* and *Plumwood Mountain*. www.jemmaborg.co.uk

Jemma's lines appear on page 3, lines 1-3, first half of line 4, page 7, lines 1-9, line 15, and page 56, lines 1-2.

Penny Boxall's collections are *Ship of the Line* (2014) and *Who Goes There?* (2016). She has won the Edwin Morgan Award, the Mslexia Poetry Competition, and a Northern Writers' Award. She has held residencies at Merton College, Oxford, Hawthornden Castle and the Chateau de Lavigny. In 2020 she is Royal Literary Fund Fellow at the University of York.

Penny's lines appear on page 61, lines 4-16.

Annie Butler studied Fine Art and Design at Carmarthen and now lives in Lampeter. Her work has appeared in the Forward Book of Poetry, and in 2017 she won the R.S. Thomas Poetry prize. She is one of The PENfro Poets based at Rhosygilwen, Pembrokeshire, and is currently working on her second poetry collection.

Annie's lines appear on page 3, lines 15-16.

Ron Carey is a poet, writer, editor and a facilitator of creative writing courses. He was born in Limerick and lives in Dublin. His poetry has won many prestigious awards. His debut poetry collection *DISTANCE* was shortlisted for the Forward Prize for Best First Collection UK and Ireland. His latest poetry collection is *Racing Down the Sun* (Revival Press).

Ron's lines appear on page 56, lines 12-18, and page 57, lines 1-2.

Graham Clifford's most recent collection, *Well*, is published by Against the Grain. His other publications are: *Computer Generated Crash Test Dummies* (Black Light Engine Room), *The Hitting Game* and *Welcome Back to the Country* (Seren).

Graham's lines appear on page 38, lines 3-9, page 39, lines 1-13, page 50, lines 10-18, and page 51, lines 1-9.

Jennifer Copley lives in Barrow-in-Furness. She has published several poetry pamphlets including *Being Haunted* which won the Cinnamon Prize in 2019, and three full collections – *Unsafe Monuments* (Arrowhead Press); *Beans in Snow;* and *Sisters* (Smokestack Press). Her fourth, *What Happens to Girls* (Pindrop Press) was published in May 2020.

Jennifer's lines appear on page 74, lines 5-11, and page 76, lines 10-18.

Martyn Crucefix's recent publications are *Cargo of Limbs* (Hercules Editions, 2019), *These Numbered Days,* translations of the poems of Peter Huchel (Shearsman, 2019) and *The Lovely Disciplines* (Seren, 2017). Currently a Royal Literary Fund fellow at Westminster University, he blogs regularly on poetry, translation and teaching: www.martyncrucefix.com

Martyn's lines appear on page 1, lines 1-4.

Kerry Darbishire lives in Cumbria where most of her poetry is rooted. She has two poetry collections (*A Lift of Wings* and *Distance Sweet on my Tongue)* with Indigo Dreams Publishing, and a biography, *Kay's Ark,* with Handstand Press. She has won and been shortlisted in several prizes including Bridport 2017. Kerry is a member of The Brewery Poets, Write on the Farm and Dove Cottage Poets.

Kerry's lines appear on page 2, lines 12-17, and page 12, second half of line

9, lines 10-12.

Cath Davies lives in Flintshire, North Wales. Her poems have been published by literary e-zines including *Nine Muses* and *Ink, Sweat & Tears*. She publishes her writing with Amazon Kindle Direct Publishing, most recently this year with a collection of short stories titled *The Data Tree*. Her work, which features the lines used in this book, will feature in the booklet *Indoors/Outdoors*, to be published by Disability Arts Cymru.

Cath's lines appear on page 63, second half of line 16, lines 17-18.

Grahame Davies is a poet, author and lyricist, who has won numerous prizes, including the Wales Book of the Year Award. A native of Coedpoeth near Wrexham, now based in Cardiff and London, he is the author of 18 books in Welsh and English, including a volume of poetry, *Lightning Beneath the Sea;* studies of Welsh literary portrayals of Judaism and Islam; a novel, *Everything Must Change*; and two books of psychogeography, *Real Wrexham (2007)* and *Real Cambridge* (forthcoming in 2020).

Grahame's lines appear on page 2, lines 3-6, page 64, lines 16-18, page 65, line 18, and page 70, lines 10-18.

Adam O. Davis is the author of *Index of Haunted Houses* (Sarabande Books, 2020) and the recipient of the 2016 George Bogin Award from the Poetry Society of America. His work has appeared in many journals, including *The Believer, The Paris Review, The Poetry Review,* and *ZYZZYVA*.

Adam's lines appear on page 5, lines 7-9.

Karen Dennison's second collection, *The Paper House*, was published by Hedgehog Poetry Press in 2019. Karen won the Indigo Dreams Collection Competition in 2011 resulting in the publication in 2012 of her first collection *Counting Rain*. Her pamphlet *Of Hearts* is forthcoming from Broken Sleep Books. As an artist, she collaborated with Abegail Morley on her pamphlet *The Memory of Water*. She is co-editor of Against the Grain Poetry Press.

Karen's lines appear on page 64, lines 11-15.

Glyn Edwards' *Vertebrae* is published by The Lonely Press. *If one day you woke up and the Eiffel Tower was gone* is taken from his second collection, *In Orbit,* in a different format. He is a teacher in North Wales.

Glyn's lines appear on page 28, lines 1-16.

Jonathan Hadas Edwards writes poetry and essays that draw on his work as a practicing healer and ritualist. Manhattan-born, he now lives far from city lights at Heartward Sanctuary, the eco-spiritual center he founded with his wife, Julia Hartsell, in North Carolina's Haw River watershed. Jonathan holds an MFA from Warren Wilson College and has published non-fiction in several periodicals, most recently *Leon Literary Review*.

Jonathan's lines appear on page 6, lines 16-18.

Will Farris is a transdisciplinary artist concerned with language and poetics across and between artistic mediums. They were the 2019 inaugural recipient of The Brannan Prize at The Poetry Project and live in New York City.

Will's lines appear on page 53, lines 12-18, and page 54, lines 1-15.

Catherine Fletcher is a Virginia-based writer. Recent work has appeared in journals such as *Hopkins Review, Entropy, New Contrast,* and *Burning House Press*, among others. She was a TWP Science and Religion fellow at Arizona State University from 2016-18 and has earned grants from Queens Council on the Arts, the Brooklyn Arts Council, and the AEV Foundation. She served for a decade as Director of Poetry Programs at the New York-based organization, City Lore, specializing in the grassroots poetry of immigrant communities. She also was Managing Director of the Los Angeles-based Ghost Road Company and served on the organizing committee of the Edge of the World Theater Festival, which highlighted the work of Los Angeles' small theatres.

Catherine's lines appear on page 3, lines 5-10.

SJ Fowler has published eight collections of poetry, five of artworks, six of collaborative poetry, and volumes of selected essays and selected collaborations. He lives in London.

SJ's lines appear on page 2, lines 7-11.

John Foy's third book of poems, *No One Leaves the World Unhurt*, won the 2020 Donald Justice Poetry Prize and will be out in early 2021 from Autumn House Press. His second book, *Night Vision*, won the New Criterion Poetry Prize and was published by St. Augustine's Press in 2016. It was also a finalist for the 2018 Poets' Prize. He lives and works in New York.

John's lines appear on page 20, lines 6-7, page 21, lines 3-11, lines 16-18, page 23, lines 14-18, and page 74, lines 1-4.

Naomi Foyle is an award-winning British-Canadian poet, science fiction novelist and essayist. Her debut collection, *The Night Pavilion*, an Autumn 2008 PBS Recommendation, was followed by *The World Cup* and *Adamantine*. *Importents*, her pamphlet of pandemic poems, is forthcoming from Waterloo Press. She is the editor of over twenty volumes of poetry.

Naomi edited a late draft of this poem.

Linda France has published eight poetry collections, including *The Toast of the Kit-Cat Club* (Bloodaxe 2005), *book of days* (Smokestack 2009) and *Reading the Flowers* (Arc 2016), longlisted for the Laurel Prize. She edited *Sixty Women Poets* (Bloodaxe 1993), won the 2013 National Poetry Competition and is a recipient of a Cholmondley Award.

Linda's lines appear on page 84, lines 17-18.

Jennifer Franklin has published two full-length poetry collections, most recently *No Small Gift* (Four Way Books, 2018). Her third book, *If Some God Shakes Your House*, will be published by Four Way Books in 2023. Her work has been published or is forthcoming in *American Poetry Review, Boston Review, Gettysburg Review, JAMA, The Nation, Paris Review,* "poem-a-day" on poets.org, and *Prairie Schooner* among others. She teaches in Manhattanville's MFA program. For the past seven years, she has taught manuscript revision at the Hudson Valley Writers' Center, where she runs the reading series, serves as Program Director, and co-edits Slapering Hol Press. She lives in New York City. Her website is jenniferfranklinpoet.com.

Jennifer's lines appear on page 87, lines 1-18.

Bashabi Fraser (PhD) is a poet, children's writer, editor, translator and academic. As a transnational writer Bashabi's work traverses continents as she writes about Scotland and India. She has authored and edited 22 books, has several published articles and chapters, both academic and creative and is widely anthologised.

Bashabi's lines appear on page 3, lines 11-14, and page 52, lines 8-9.

Beatrice Garland has had a long career in the National Health Service as clinician, teacher and researcher. She has published two books of poetry: *The Invention of Fireworks* (short-listed for the Forward Prize for best First Collection), and *The Drum*. She won the National Poetry Competition in 2001, and the Strokestown Prize in 2002. She lives in London.

Beatrice's lines appear on page 85, lines 1-18.

Lesley Glaister's first novel was published in 1990 and since then she's published 14 further adult novels, the first in a trilogy of YA novels and numerous short stories. Several of her plays have been broadcasted on BBC Radio 4 and her first stage play, *Bird Calls*, was performed at Sheffield's Crucible Studio Theatre in 2004. Mariscat Press published her pamphlets of poetry *Visiting The Animal*, in 2015, and *Nub*, in 2019.

Lesley's lines appear on page 68, lines 2-5.

John Glenday's third collection, *Grain* (Picador, 2009), was a Poetry Book Society Recommendation and was shortlisted for both the Ted Hughes Award and the Griffin International Poetry Prize. His fourth collection, *The Golden Mean* (Picador, 2015), was shortlisted for the Saltire Scottish Poetry Book of the Year and won the 2015 Roehampton Poetry Prize. Picador will publish his Selected Poems in 2020.

John's lines appear on page 40, lines 1-2, first half of line 3, lines 6-7, second half of line 13, line 14, and page 59, lines 1-7.

Rebecca Goss is the author of three full-length poetry collections, most recently *Girl* (Carcanet, 2019).

Rebecca's lines appear on page 49, lines 1-18.

Angela Graham's poetry has appeared in *The North, The Honest Ulsterman, The Interpreter's House, Poetry in Motion Anthology 2020, North Star, The Blue Nib* and elsewhere, and imminently in *Places of Poetry, The Lonely Crowd* and *The Stony Thursday Book.* Her short story collection *A City Burning* will be published by Seren Books in 2020. Her poem appeared on http://pendemic.ie/an-irish-covid-gift-a-poem-by-angela-graham/

Angela's lines appear on page 35, lines 7-15.

Mark Granier's poems have appeared in various outlets in Ireland and the UK over the years, including *The New Statesman, Poetry Ireland Review, The TLS, Poetry Review* and, recently, Carol Ann Duffy's *Write Where We Are NOW* Covid 19 project for Manchester University. His work has also been broadcast on RTE. Prizes and awards include the Vincent Buckley Poetry Prize and two Patrick and Katherine Kavanagh Fellowships. His fifth collection, *Ghostlight: New & Selected Poems*, was published by Salmon Poetry in May 2017.

Mark's lines appear on page 42, lines 8-18, page 43, lines 1-2, and page 67, lines 1-8.

Andrew Greig is the author of many books. His recent non-fiction memoirs are *At the Loch of the Green Corrie* and *You Know What You Could Be* (with Mike Heron); latest novel *Fair Helen*; most recent collection of poems *Later That Day* (Polygon).

Andrew's lines appear on page 57, lines 3-9, and page 60, lines 7-9.

Carl Griffin's first poetry collection, *Throat of Hawthorn*, was published by Indigo Dreams Publishing in 2019. Though born in Stockton-on-Tees, he has spent most of his life living in each of the South Wales cities, places that inspire many of his poems. Twitter: @0CarlGriffin0

Carl's individual lines appear on page 1, lines 13-14, lines 17-18, page 2, lines 1-2, line 18, page 3, second half of line 4, lines 17-18, page 4, line 3, page 8, line 11, page 9, lines 8-18, page 11, line 14-18, page 12, line 13, page 17, line 18, page 19, lines 9-11, page 20, line 3, line 12, page 22, lines 13-15, page 29, line 9, page 33, lines 2-3, page 41, lines 5-9, lines 15-18, page 45, lines 5-6, page 52, line 12, first half of line 13, line 17, page 53, lines 10-11, page 57, lines 16-18, page 58, lines 1-3, page 59, line 8, lines 14-16, page 61, lines 17-18, page 68, lines 15-18, page 69, lines 1-11, page 71, lines 1-16, page 72, lines 1-18, page 74, line 18, page 83, lines 3-6, page 90, lines 12-13, line 16, and page 91, lines 15-16.

Seán Griffin's writing is largely available online should it be sought. Seán is hard at work reading manga and writing their first collection.

Seán's lines appear on page 88, lines 9-18, and page 89 lines 1-9.

Philip Gross has published some twenty collections of poetry, most recently, *Between The Islands* (Bloodaxe, 2020). He won the T.S. Eliot Prize in 2009 and a Cholmondeley Award in 2017. He is a keen collaborator – with artist Valerie Coffin Price on *A Fold In The River* (Seren, 2015), with poet Lesley Saunders on *A Part of the Main* (Mulfran, 2018) and with scientists on *Dark Sky Park* (Otter-Barry, 2018). www.philipgross.co.uk

Philip's lines appear on page 4, lines 10-16, page 5, lines 17-18, page 6, lines 1-4, page 12, lines 14-18, page 13, lines 1-9, page 20, second half of line 14, lines 15-18, page 21, lines 1-2, page 34, second half of line 14, lines 15-18, and page 35, lines 1-6.

Rachel Hadas is the author of many books of poetry, essays, and translations. Recent poetry collections include *The Golden Road* (2012), *Questions in the Vestibule* (2016), and *Poems for Camilla* (2018). *Love and Dread* is forthcoming in the fall of 2020, and a prose collection, *Piece by Piece*, in 2021. Rachel lives in New York City and Vermont, where she hopes to stay for the foreseeable future. Since 2013, she and her husband Shalom Gorewitz have been marrying poetry and video: www.rachelandshalomshow.com

Rachel's lines appear on page 1, lines 5-12, page 43, lines 13-18, page 44, lines 3-9, and page 84, lines 12-16.

Matthew Haigh is a poet from Cardiff. His debut collection, *Death Magazine*, was published with Salt in 2019 and longlisted for the Polari First Book Prize 2020. In the same year he published a pamphlet, *Black Jam*, with Broken Sleep Books. Matthew's poetry was highly commended in the Forward Prizes 2020.

Matthew's lines appear on page 54, lines 16-18.

Jean Hall's poems have appeared in several anthologies and poetry publications, and she was recently chosen for the Cambridge Writing Retreat's podcast of 30 poets.

Jean's lines appear on page 19, lines 1-8.

Myronn Hardy is the author of, most recently, *Radioactive Starlings*, published by Princeton University Press (2017). His poems have appeared in journals such as the *New York Times Magazine, jubilat, the Virginia Quarterly Review*, and elsewhere.

Myronn's lines appear on page 23, lines 1-9, and page 26, lines 13-16.

Rob Hindle has published several collections of poetry with Templar, Smokestack and Longbarrow Press. The most recent, *The Grail Roads* (Longbarrow, 2018), was chosen as The New European's Book of the Year. *The Tapestry Makers of Flanders*, from that collection, appears in The Forward Book of Poetry 2020.

Rob's lines appear on page 6, second half of line 11, lines 12-15, and page 14, lines 17-18.

Sarah Hymas lives by Morecambe Bay, England. Her writing appears in print, multimedia exhibits, as lyrics, installations and on stage. She also makes artistbooks and immersive walks. @sarahhymas

Sarah's lines appear on page 16, second half of line 1, line 2, page 18, lines 15-16, page 62, lines 8-9, and page 91, lines 10-14.

Sarah James/Leavesley's books include *How to Grow Matches* (Against The Grain Poetry Press, 2018), shortlisted in the International Rubery Book Awards 2018 and finalist in the Eyelands Book Awards 2019, and *The Magnetic Diaries* (Knives Forks and Spoons Press, 2015), highly commended in the Forward Prizes. She runs V. Press, a poetry and flash fiction imprint. Her lines were extracted from her poem *Katherina's Hair*

Chronicles, first published in *Abridged 0-19 Eris* in May 2020. : www.sarah-james.co.uk

Sarah's lines appear on page 31, lines 1-4.

Pam Job lives in Wivenhoe, Essex. She has co-edited six poetry anthologies, and had a poem included in a new Oratorio, *The Affirming Flame*, premiered at Snape Maltings in 2019, along with poems by Siegfried Sassoon and Charles Hamilton Sorley. She is working towards a first collection.

Pam's lines appear on page 29, lines 1-8.

Troy Jollimore is the author of three books of poems: *Tom Thomson in Purgatory* (2006), *At Lake Scugog* (2011), and *Syllabus of Errors* (2015). *Tom Thomson in Purgatory* won the National Book Critics Circle Award, and in 2013 he received a Guggenheim fellowship. His poems have been or will be published in the *New Yorker, McSweeney's, Poetry, Best American Poetry 2020,* and elsewhere.

Troy's lines appear on page 8, lines 1-9.

Adrianne Kalfopoulou is the author of three poetry collections, most recently *A History of Too Much* (2018). She has also published two prose collections, including *Ruin, Essays in Exilic Living* (2014). She is currently the 2020-2021 McGee Professor of Creative Writing at Davidson College.

Adrianne's lines appear on page 63, lines 5-13, and page 79, lines 9-16.

David M. Katz is the author of four books of poetry: *In Praise of Manhattan, Stanzas on Oz,* and *Claims of Home (*all published by Dos Madres Press), and *The Warrior in the Forest* (House of Keys Press). Poems of his have appeared in *PN Review, Poetry, The New Criterion*, and elsewhere. He lives in New York City. (davidmkatzpoet.com)

David's lines appear on page 48, lines 1-16.

Yusef Komunyakaa's books of poetry include *Neon Vernacular,* for which he received the Pulitzer Prize, *The Chameleon Couch, The Emperor of Water Clocks,* and *Everyday Mojo Songs of Earth (*forthcoming 2021). His honors include the William Faulkner Prize (Université Rennes, France), the Ruth Lilly Poetry Prize, and the Wallace Stevens Award. His plays, performance art and libretti include *The Deacons, Gilgamesh: a verse play,* and *Somewhere Near Here (Bright Darkness).* He teaches at New York University.

Yusef's lines appear on page 80, lines 1-18, and page 81, lines 1-15.

Aaron Lembo was the winning librettist at the 2017 Rosamond Prize and his librettos have been performed at the Leeds Lieder Festival and at the International Anthony Burgess Foundation. He has taught English in China, Spain and Vietnam. Currently, he lives in his home county of Kent where he is working on his debut collection.

Aaron's lines appear on page 24, lines 1-18, and page 25, lines 1-18.

Christopher Levenson, who lives in Vancouver, BC (Canada), has published twelve books of poetry. In 1960 he was first winner of the Eric Gregory prize. A subsequent book, *Arriving at night*, won the Ottawa's Archibald Lampman Award, while *Night Vision* in 2014 was short-listed for the Governor General's Award for poetry. He was co-founder and first editor of the influential *Arc* poetry magazine.

Christopher's lines appear on page 16, lines 12-16, page 17, line 13, and page 19, lines 12-17.

Thyrza Leyshon lives and works in Essex. Her work has appeared in a range of publications including *The Forward Book of Poetry 2020* and the anthology *She Will Soar,* published by Macmillan in the September of that year.

Thyrza's lines appear on page 84, lines 1-9.

Ele-Beth Little is a postgraduate creative writing student, book blogger and Psychology and Philosophy teacher from the North of England. Her work has been published by Bone and Ink press and Paraphilia Press, and she is currently working on her first novel. The full piece can be read here: https://impenetrablenight.wordpress.com/2020/03/18/contained-march-18th-2020/   Twitter: @elebethx

Ele-Beth's lines appear on page 56, lines 3-9.

Lorraine Mariner has published two collections with Picador, *Furniture* (2009) and *There Will Be No More Nonsense* (2014). She has twice been shortlisted in the Forward Prizes, for Best Poem and Best First Collection, and for the Seamus Heaney Centre Poetry Prize. Her latest publication is the chapbook *Anchorage* (2020) with Grey Suit Editions.

Lorraine's lines appear on page 60, lines 10-18, and page 62, lines 5-7.

Peter Marra's latest poetry collection is *Random Crucifixions: Obsessions, Dolls and Maniac Cameras* (Hammer & Anvil Books). His novel, *A Naked Kiss from a Broken Doll*, is also to be published by Hammer & Anvil Books. He was Danse Macabre Magazine's Artist-in-residence for 2018. Twitter: @Angelferox Instagram: peterdmarra

Peter's lines appear on page 79, second half of line 6, lines 7-8.

Tim Mayo's first full-length collection, *The Kingdom of Possibilities* (Mayapple Press, 2009), was a finalist for the 2009 May Swenson Award. His second volume of poems, *Thesaurus of Separation* (Phoenicia Publishing 2016) was a finalist for the 2017 Montaigne Medal and a finalist for the 2017 Eric Hoffer Book Award. His poems have received seven Pushcart Prize nominations. He lives in Southern Vermont (USA), where he works in a Mental Hospital.

Tim's lines appear on page 41, lines 10-14, and page 63, lines 14-15, first half of line 16.

Chris McCabe's work crosses artforms and genres including poetry, fiction, non-fiction, drama and visual art. His work has been shortlisted for the Ted Hughes Award and the Republic of Consciousness Prize. His most recent books are *The Triumph of Cancer* (Penned in the Margins, 2018), and *Mud* (Henningham Family Press, 2019). He works as the National Poetry Librarian at Southbank Centre's National Poetry Library.

Chris's lines appear on page 33, lines 4-6

Richie McCaffery lives in Alnwick, Northumberland. His most recent poetry pamphlet is *First Hare* (Mariscat Press, 2020).

Richie's lines appear on page 21, lines 12-15, page 23, lines 10-13, page 32, lines 9-10, page 33, line 1, lines 7-9, page 44, lines 1-2, and page 45, lines 1-4.

Michael McKimm lives in East London. An Eric Gregory Award winner, his publications include *Still This Need* (Heaventree Press, 2009) and *Fossil Sunshine* (Worple Press, 2013) and he has edited the anthologies *MAP: Poems after William Smith's Geological Map of 1815* and *The Tree Line: Poems for Trees, Woods & People* (both Worple Press).

Michael's lines appear on page 46, lines 1-18, page 51, lines 10-16, first half of line 17, page 52, lines 1-7, page 53, lines 1-9, page 82, lines 15-16, and page 83, lines 7-18.

Rafael Mendes is a poet and translator whose work has appeared on The Poetry Programme, The Irish Times, FLARE and on *Writing Home: The New Irish Poets* (Dedalus Press, 2019). He also has poems published in Brazil and Portugal. He's a member of NIC writers group at The Irish Writers Centre.

Rafael's lines appear on page 60, lines 1-6.

Matt Merritt is a poet and journalist from Leicester. His poetry collections are *The Elephant Tests* (Nine Arches, 2013), *hydrodaktulopsychicharmonica* (Nine Arches, 2010) and *Troy Town* (Arrowhead, 2008), and he is the author of a natural history memoir, *A Sky Full of Birds* (Rider Books, 2016). He blogs at polyolbion.blogspot.com

Matt's lines appear on page 66, lines 1-18.

Bruce Meyer is author of sixty three books of poetry, short stories, flash fiction, and non-fiction with seven more forthcoming in the next three years. He lives in Barrie, Ontario.

Bruce's lines appear on page 73, lines 1-18.

Kathy Miles is a poet and short story writer living in West Wales. Her third collection of poetry, *Gardening With Deer*, was published by Cinnamon Press in 2016. She is a co-editor of *The Lampeter Review*, and is a previous winner of the Bridport Prize. Her fourth collection of poetry, *Bone House*, will be published by Indigo Dreams later this year.

Kathy's lines appear on page 55, lines 1-5, page 57, lines 14-15, and page 58, lines 4-18.

Jessica Mookherjee's first full collection, *Flood*, was published in 2018 by Cultured Llama. Her second collection, *Tigress,* was published in 2019 by Nine Arches Press. Jessica is a board member of the Poetry Society and co-editor of Against the Grain Poetry Press.

Jessica's lines appear on page 62, lines 1-4.

Abigail Morley's fifth collection, *The Unmapped Woman*, is published by Nine Arches Press. Her debut, *How to Pour Madness into a Teacup*, was shortlisted for the Forward Prize Best First Collection. She is a co-editor at Against the Grain Press and editor of The Poetry Shed.

Abigail's lines appear on page 64, lines 1-9, and page 65, lines 1-17.

Katrina Naomi was born and raised in Margate, Kent and lives in Cornwall. Her third full collection, *Wild Persistence*, was published by Seren in June 2020. She was the first writer-in-residence at the Brontë Parsonage Museum, and tutors for Arvon, the Poetry School, Ty Newydd and the Poetry Society. She holds a PhD in Creative Writing from Goldsmiths (her research is on violence in contemporary poetry). She recently received an Author's Foundation Award from the Society of Authors. https://www.katrinanaomi.co.uk/

Katrina's lines appear on page 37, lines 10-18, and page 38, lines 1-2.

Lizzie Nunnery is an award-winning scriptwriter, working in theatre, radio and film. Work includes *Intemperance* (Liverpool Everyman, 2007) which was shortlisted for the Meyer-Whitworth Award, and *Narvik* (UK Tour 2017, Norwegian tour 2019) which won Best New Play at the UK Theatre Awards. Lizzie is also a songwriter, singer and musician, performing regularly with composer Vidar Norheim. Some of Lizzie's lines used in this book were originally part of a short story, *Little Bird*, commissioned by Culture Liverpool.

Lizzie's lines appear on page 32, lines 14-15, page 35, lines 16-18, and page 36, lines 1-9.

Jean O'Brien lives in Dublin, Ireland and has five collections of poetry published. Her latest is her *New & Collected Fish on a Bicycle* (Salmon Publishing). An award-winning poet, she has won prizes in the Arvon Inter. Poetry Competition (W) & the Fish International (W) and the Forward Prize (H.C.). She was a 2017/18 Patrick Kavanagh Fellow. She tutors in creative writing/poetry.

Jean's lines appear on page 51, second half of line 17, Line 18.

Sean O'Brien's tenth collection of poems, *It Says Here*, is published by Picador in autumn 2020. His work has received the T.S. Eliot and Forward Prizes. He is Professor of Creative Writing at Newcastle University.

Sean's lines appear on page 91, lines 1-8.

Alasdair Paterson's most recent collections are *Elsewhere Or Thereabouts* (Shearsman Books 2014), *My Life As A Mad King* (Oystercatcher 2016) and *Silent Years* (Flarestack Poets 2017). Born in Edinburgh, he began writing poetry in Liverpool in the 1970s and won an Eric Gregory Award in 1975. After a 20 year sabbatical, he started to write again in 2007. He lives in Exeter, where he organizes and presents the monthly Uncut Poets reading series.

Alasdair's lines appear on page 5, lines 13-16, page 31, lines 5-18, page 32, lines 1-8, page 33, lines 10-18, page 34, lines 1-8, page 38, lines 14-15, page 45, lines 7-9, page 52, lines 10-11, second half of line 13, lines 14-15, and page 63, lines 1-4.

Vic Pickup previously won the Café Writers competition with her poem about a Bosnian chicken, and was recently shortlisted for National Poetry Day's #speakyourtruth competition. She is currently seeking a publisher for her debut pamphlet. www.vicpickup.com

Vic's lines appear on page 1, lines 15-16.

John Priestly has had work published in various sources - *Southlight*, Hedgehog Press etc., and is currently finishing a collaborative piece with David Mark Williams. He was shortlisted in 2019 for the Dumfries & Galloway new voices award. In Scotland, where he lives, he runs a small Poetry group which has published 10 pamphlets with the 11th awaiting printing.

John's lines appear on page 59, lines 11-12.

Edward Ragg won the 2012 Cinnamon Press Poetry Award. His collections to date, all with Cinnamon Press, are *A Force That Takes* (2013), *Holding Unfailing* (2017) and *Exploring Rights* (2020). His work has been anthologised in *New Poetries IV* (Carcanet, 2007), the *2014 Forward Book of Poetry* (Faber, 2013) and elsewhere. Edward's major critical work is *Wallace Stevens and the Aesthetics of Abstraction* (Cambridge University Press, 2010). www.edwardragg.com

Edward's lines appear on page 47, lines 1-9.

Jeremy Reed has published over fifty books of poetry, fiction and non-fiction, and performed all over London and Europe as Jeremy Reed and the Ginger Light, as a collaboration with the musician Itchy Ear. The Independent called him 'British poetry's glam, spangly, shape-shifting answer to David Bowie.'

Jeremy's lines appear on page 29, lines 12-18, and page 30, lines 1-18.

Christopher Riesco lives and works in Manchester. He occasionally publishes in magazines.

Christopher's lines appear on page 62, 10-18.

Eléna Rivera's third full-length collection of poetry *Scaffolding* (2017) was published by Princeton University Press in the Princeton Series of Contemporary Poets. Her book of poems, *Epic Series*, is forthcoming from Shearsman Books. She received a National Endowment for the Arts Literature Fellowship in Translation and was a recent recipient of fellowships from MacDowell (2020), and a Trelex Paris Poetry Residency (2019).

Eléna's lines appear on page 7, lines 10-14, lines 16-18.

Danny Rivers is a member of Roundel, a Poetry Society Stanza, based in Tonbridge. He has previously contributed to *Links in the Chain: Five Years of Roundel*, LacunaPublish, Great Britain, 2017 and *Write to be counted: An Anthology of Poetry to Uphold Human Rights*, edited by Jacci Bulman, Nicola Jackson and Kathleen Jones, The Book Mill, UK, 2017.

Danny's lines appear on page 19, line 18, and page 20, lines 1-2.

Chrys Salt is a poet with roots deeply planted in the theatre. She has produced four full poetry collections and given readings in the USA, Canada, France, Germany, Finland, India and Australia. She has been the recipient of various Awards and Bursaries, including one for research in Yukon for her most recent collection *Skookum Jim and The Klondike Gold Rush* (Indigo Dreams Publishing 2020). She was awarded an MBE for Services to The Arts in the Queen's Birthday Honour's List 2014. www. chryssalt.com

Chrys's lines appear on page 4, line 1, and page 10, lines 12-15.

John Sewell lives in Shropshire. Two previous collections, from Littlewood and Cape, are now out of print. Fair Acre Press are publishing a new collection in 2021.

John's lines appear on page 8, line 10, page 9, lines 1-7, and page 42, lines 1-4.

Peter Sirr has published ten poetry collections, of which the most recent are *The Gravity Wave* (2019), a Poetry Book Society recommendation, and *Sway* (2016), versions of poems from the troubadour tradition. *The Thing Is* (2009), was awarded the Michael Hartnett Prize in 2011. His novel for children, *Black Wreath*, was published in 2014. His radio dramas are broadcast on RTE, the Irish national broadcaster. He lives in Dublin.

Peter's lines appear on page 20, lines 4-5, line 8, and page 74, lines 12-17.

Maria Sledmere is a poet and critic living in Glasgow. She is a member of A+E Collective, editor for SPAM Press and occasional music journalist. Recent publications include *Rainbow Arcadia* (Face Press) and *infra·structure* – with Katy Lewis Hood (Broken Sleep). Forthcoming works include *chlorophyllia* (OrangeApple Press), *varnish // cache* (If a Leaf Falls) and *neutral milky halo* (Guillemot Press).

Maria's lines appear on page 41, lines 1-4, and page 61, lines 1-3.

Austin Smith is the author of two collections, *Almanac* and *Flyover Country*, both published through the Princeton Series of Contemporary Poets. He was a Wallace Stegner Fellow in fiction at Stanford University, where he teaches creative writing. He received the Amy Lowell Traveling Scholarship for 2020-2021, and lives in Schapville, Illinois.

Austin's lines appear on page 42, lines 5-7.

Gerard Smyth is a poet, critic and journalist whose work has appeared in journals in Ireland, Britain and the United States as well as in translation since the 1960s. He has published ten collections, including *The Sundays of Eternity* (Dedalus Press, 2020), and *The Fullness of Time: New and Selected Poems* (Dedalus Press, 2010). He is co-editor, with Pat Boran, of *If Ever You Go: A Map of Dublin in Poetry and Song* (Dedalus Press) which was Dublin's One City One Book in 2014. He is a member of Aosdána (Ireland's affiliation of artists).

Gerard's lines appear on page 22, lines 1-9, page 27, lines 10-18, and page 44, second half of line 16, lines 17-18.

Sue Spiers lives in Hampshire with her covid companion, husband John Ward. Her first collection is called *Jiggle Sac* and a new collection is underway (containing the haiku used in this long poem), *Plague - A Season of Senryu*. Sue tweets @spiropoetry.

Sue's lines appear on page 26, lines 17-18.

Julian Stannard's books include *The Street of Perfect Love* (Worple Press, 2014), *What were you thinking?* (CB Editions, 2016), *Sottoripa: Genoese Poems* (Canneto Editore, 2018), and *Heat Wave* (Salt, 2020). Stannard's study of Basil Bunting was published by the Liverpool University Press (2014). He is a Reader in English and Creative Writing at the University of Winchester (UK).

Julian's lines appear on page 27, lines 1-3, first half of line 4, lines 8-9, page 36, lines 10-18, page 37, lines 1-9, and page 86, lines 10-18.

Alina Stefanescu was born in Romania and lives in Birmingham, Alabama, with her partner and several intense mammals. Her books include *Every Mask I Tried On* (Brighthorse Books, 2018). She serves as Poetry Editor for Pidgeonholes, Poetry Editor for *Random Sample Review*, Poetry Reviewer for *Up the Staircase Quarterly,* and Co-Director of PEN America's Birmingham Chapter. www.alinastefanescuwriter.com

Alina's lines appear on page 4, line 2, lines 4-9.

Arundhathi Subramaniam is the award-winning author of twelve books of poetry and prose. She lives between Bombay, New York, Chennai and Coimbatore. Her book, *When God is a Traveller* (Bloodaxe Books, 2014) won the inaugural Khushwant Singh Prize in India, the International Piero Bigongiari Award in Italy, and was the Season Choice of the Poetry Book Society, shortlisted for the T.S. Eliot Prize. Her most recent book, *Love Without a Story*, was published in India by Westland Amazon in 2019, and is forthcoming from Bloodaxe Books.

Arundhathi's lines appear on page 22, lines 10-12, and page 27, second half of Line 4, Lines 5-7.

Hideko Sueoka is a Japanese poet and translator living in Tokyo. She was the winner of the 2013 Troubadour International Poetry Competition and her winning poem was highly commended in the Forward Prize 2014. Her debut poetry chapbook was out from Clare Songbirds Publishing House (USA) in 2018. Her blog is *CHEERFUL NOISE as in a poem.*

Hideko's lines appear on page 89, lines 10-18.

George Szirtes's *Reel* (2004) won the T.S. Eliot Prize for which he has been twice shortlisted since. His latest is *Mapping the Delta* (2016). His memoir *The Photographer at Sixteen* appeared in 2019.

George's lines appear on page 8, lines 12-18, page 17, lines 14-16, page 26, lines 1-12, page 34, lines 9-13, first half of Line 14, page 40, second half of line 3, lines 4-7, page 50, lines 1-9, page 59, lines 9-10, line 13, page 67, lines 9-13, page 69, lines 12-18, page 70, lines 1-9, page 75, lines 1-9, page 76, lines 1-9, page 77, lines 1-18, page 78, lines 1-18, page 79, lines 1-4, page 90, lines 9-11.

Simon Tin was born in Sunderland, wrote songs in South London and found poetry in West Yorkshire. He is currently working on his first collection.

Simon's lines appear on page 84, lines 10-11.

Csilla Toldy published three titles with Lapwing Belfast: *Red roots - Orange Sky* (2013), *The Emigrant Woman's Tale* (2015) and *Vertical Montage* (2018). Her short story collection, *Angel Fur and other stories,* was published by Stupor Mundi in 2019. She makes video poems: www. csillatoldy.co.uk

Csilla's lines appear on page 79 Line 5, first half of line 6.

Helen Tookey lives in Liverpool. She has published two full-length poetry collections with Carcanet Press, *Missel-Child* (2014, shortlisted for the Seamus Heaney Prize) and *City of Departures* (2019, shortlisted for the Forward Prize for Best Collection), and is currently working on a third.

Helen's lines appear on page 16, first half of line 1, lines 3-11, 17-18, page 17, lines 1-12, page 18, lines 4-14, lines 17-18.

Olivia Tuck's pamphlet, *Things Only Borderlines Know,* is out now with Black Rabbit Press. She also has work forthcoming in *Tears in the Fence,* where she works with the editing team as an intern whilst studying for a BA in Creative Writing at Bath Spa University. Find her on Twitter: @ livtuckwrites

Olivia edited an early draft of this poem.

Julian Turner was born in Cheshire and his first collection (*Crossing the Outskirts*) was published by Anvil in 2002. This was short-listed for the Forward Prize Best First Collection Prize and was a Poetry Book Society recommendation. His second volume, *Orphan Sites* (2006), and third, *Planet-Struck* (2011), were also published by Anvil. *Planet-Struck* was a PBS recommendation. Julian was a grateful recipient of a Northern Writers' Award in 2014. A fourth collection, *Desolate Market* (2018), was published by Carcanet.

Julian's lines appear on page 4, lines 17-18, page 5, lines 1-6, 10-12, page 6, lines 5-10, first half of line 11, page 10, lines 1-12, page 11, lines 1-8, page 12, lines 1-8, first half of line 9, page 13, lines 10-18, page 14, lines 1-13, page 15, lines 1-16, page 22, lines 16-18, page 29, lines 10-11, page 38, lines 10-13, lines 16-18, page 43, line 9, page 47, lines 10-18, page 52, line 16, line 18, page 57, lines 10-13, page 67, lines 14-18, page 68, line 1, lines 6-14, page 75, lines 10-18, page 81, lines 16-18, page 82, lines 1-9, lines 17-18, page 83, lines 1-3, page 88, lines 1-8, page 90, lines 1-8, lines 14-15, lines 17-18.

Phil Vernon lives in Kent. His first full collection *Poetry After Auschwitz* is due from Sentinel in 2020.

Phil's lines appear on page 10, lines 16-18, and page 11, lines 9-13.

Steve Walter's Dad was a poet, his Mum a watercolour artist. Steve has performed at the Brighton and Edinburgh Festival Fringes, based on his first book: *Fast Train Approaching...* a powerful, yet good humoured, account of life during and after breakdown and recovery. His second pamphlet of poetry, *When the Change Came,* was published by Indigo Dreams in 2016, and his long poem, *Gaia 2020,* is published by Making Connections Matter.

Steve's lines appear on page 20, line 13, first half of line 14.

Bogusia Wardein is a Polish poet. Her work has appeared in various magazines including *The Rialto* and *Poetry Wales,* as well as the anthologies *Hallelujah for 50ft Women* (Bloodaxe, 2015) and *Writing Home* (Dedalus, 2019). She was the winner of the New Zealand Poetry Society 2018 Competition and has been commended or shortlisted in the Bridport

Prize, the Plough Prize and the Hippocrates Prize. www.bogusiawardein.com

Bogusia's lines appear on page 55, lines 6-18, and page 56, lines 10-11.

Sarah Westcott's first collection *Slant Light* was published by Pavilion Poetry, an imprint of Liverpool University Press, in 2016. A poem from the book was Highly Commended in the 2017 Forward Prizes. Her debut pamphlet *Inklings* (Flipped Eye) was a Poetry Book Society pamphlet choice in 2013. Her second collection is due with Pavilion Poetry next year.

Sarah's lines appear on page 43, lines 3-8, page 44, lines 10-15, first half of line 16, page 45, lines 10-18, page 82, lines 10-14, and page 91, line 9.

Charles Wilkinson's most recent poetry collections are *Ag & Au* (Flarestack Poets, 2013) and *The Glazier's Choice* (Eyewear, 2019). He lives in Powys, Wales.

Charles's lines appear on page 39, lines 14-18.

Keith S. Wilson is the author of *Fieldnotes on Ordinary Love* (Copper Canyon, 2019). A Cave Canem fellow, he teaches poetry and game design, and lives in Chicago, Illinois.

Keith's lines appear on page 40, lines 10-12, first half of line 13, lines 15-16.

Gareth Writer-Davies is from Brecon, Wales. He was shortlisted for the Bridport Prize (2014 and 2017), and his publications include *Bodies* (2015) and *Cry Baby* (2017), both via Indigo Dreams, as well as *The Lover's Pinch* (2018) and *The End* (2019), both via Arenig Press. He was a Hawthornden Fellow (2019).

Gareth's lines appear on page 86, lines 1-9.